BETTER THAN BEST PRACTICES

PRINCIPLES FOR INTENTIONAL UX DESIGN

A. Robert Hinson

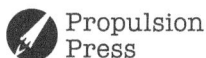

Propulsion
Press

Contents

Preface   3

Introduction   5

1. Best Practices Are Tools, Not Rules   9

2. Context Is King   15

3. Friction Isn't the Enemy   31

4. Designing with Awareness, Not Au-   39
   topilot

5. The CUE Framework™   51

Conclusion   59

Preface

After more than two decades designing and building digital products, I've seen best practices help teams move faster and align more easily. But I've often wrestled with colleagues who clung to prescriptive formulas, even when it was clear those approaches didn't fit the problem. I've seen best practices misapplied, misunderstood and weaponized—used as shortcuts when what was really needed was curiosity, context and courage.

Better Than Best Practices isn't a rejection of standards. It's a challenge to use them more wisely.

I wrote this for designers who want to move beyond default thinking. For those who do everything "by the book" and still feel like something's missing. And for anyone who's ever followed a prescribed best practice, only to watch it fall flat.

This is not a textbook. It's a conversation starter. A set of provocations. A push to pause before pressing forward.

There's no checklist at the end. No one-size-fits-all solution. Just a call to think more clearly, question more freely and design more intentionally.

Let's begin.

—A. Robert Hinson
2025

Introduction

The Problem with "Best Practices"

In every field, there is comfort in the idea of a "best practice." It suggests that someone else has already done the hard work, tested the options and found the most effective solution. In UX, best practices often come packaged in lists, frameworks and blog posts, ready to copy, paste and deploy. They promise clarity amid complexity, speed in decision-making and safety through consensus.

But here's the problem: what's "best" in one context can be mediocre or even harmful in another.

Origins and Evolution

The term "best practices" has roots in early 20th-century management theory. Frederick Winslow Taylor, the father of scientific management, believed in finding "the one best way" to perform a task, typically on a factory floor. The idea was simple: study the work, optimize it and replicate the method to boost efficiency and minimize error.

By the late 20th century, the concept had spread from assembly lines to boardrooms. The rise of corporate benchmarking in the 1980s and '90s encouraged companies to look outward at industry leaders, competitors or case studies to identify repeatable strategies. Consulting firms championed these findings, packaging them as "best practices" for adoption across sectors:

healthcare, education, government, software development. Eventually, UX and digital product design followed suit.

And why not? In a fast-moving, ambiguous industry, a best practice can feel like a lifeline. A safe bet when the pressure's on.

But we must remember where they come from. UX best practices are born from patterns and data, but they're not universal truths. They come from specific environments, shaped by particular users, products, goals and constraints. When we treat them as rules instead of tools, we risk designing by default rather than making conscious, thoughtful decisions.

This book is about helping you ask better questions, not just find better answers. We'll examine the forces that shape design such as technological shifts, human behavior and business priorities, and offer practical ways to make informed choices in the face of uncertainty. Best practices aren't the enemy. But they are a *guide* and not a mandate.

Chapter One

Best Practices Are Tools, Not Rules

Best practices represent collective experience, but they're no substitute for your own judgment. They can save us time, help us avoid common pitfalls and offer a sense of direction when we're unsure how to proceed. However, they're not sacred, not the law and not even always right.

Think of best practices as tools in a toolbox. Just because you own a hammer doesn't mean every problem is a nail. A screwdriver isn't "better" than a wrench; it's just better for certain jobs. Likewise, best practices are only as good as the context in which you use them.

Distilled Knowledge, Not Absolute Truths

What we call best practices are often the hard-won lessons of those who came before us. Patterns that worked well in specific situations and proved themselves over time. But like all heuristics, they're shortcuts. They carry assumptions. They work until they don't.

Take the common advice to prioritize everything "above the fold," the idea that users won't scroll, so all key content must be visible without scrolling. It may sound reasonable. But studies have shown that users *do* scroll, especially when the design offers clear cues and a compelling reason to continue. Forcing everything into the top of the page can lead to cluttered, overwhelming layouts that hurt comprehension and engagement.

When Best Practices Go Wrong

History is full of examples where best practices were followed to the letter and still failed.

Consider infinite scroll. It started as a best practice for increasing engagement, removing page breaks so users could keep exploring content without interruption. But in task-driven contexts, like ecommerce or search, it can frustrate users. They lose their place, can't bookmark content, and struggle to compare options. A practice designed for delight becomes a source of friction and frustration.

Or take progressive disclosure. The idea that showing only essential information up front helps users focus and avoid becoming overwhelmed. In theory, it's smart. In practice, it *can* backfire. When too much is hidden, users may have to hunt for answers or miss key details altogether. What starts as a strategy for clarity ends up creating confusion.

Use the Right Tool for the Job

To work effectively, we need to approach best practices like a seasoned craftsperson: aware of the tools, familiar with their strengths and limitations and willing to improvise when the job demands it.

Best practices are not the job itself. They're a starting point. A scaffolding. A hypothesis to test, not a conclusion to assume.

Every project is different. Every audience brings new needs. Every constraint reshapes the field. The real skill is knowing when to use a best practice, how to adapt it and when to set it aside completely.

***

Jacob's Law: A Timeless Truism

Jacob's Law is a cornerstone of UX best practices, stating that "users spend most of their time on other sites, so they prefer your site to work the same way as all the others they already know."

This principle stands as a simple, powerful truth. Users bring with them a lifetime of experiences with familiar interfaces and they naturally gravitate toward designs that match their established habits. In this light, Jacob's Law isn't just a guideline but rather an observation of human behavior at its core. It reminds us that predictable layouts and familiar interactions can drastically reduce cognitive friction and make digital experiences more intuitive.

By embracing Jacob's Law, designers tap into a shared baseline of user expectations. When you design a navigation menu, a search bar or even the placement of a shopping cart, you're building on a collective language of interface design. This common framework is one of the most valuable tools in our design toolbox.

There may be moments where deviating from norms makes sense. The real strength of Jacob's Law, however, lies in its simplicity—a truism that, when understood correctly, adds reliability and comfort to a user's journey without dictating every design choice.

Ultimately, best practices like Jacob's Law still serve as a starting point, a reminder of the core realities of user behavior to be adapted thoughtfully based on the unique requirements of each project.

Chapter Two

Context Is King

A best practice is only meaningful if it works in the situation you're designing for. Every decision in UX, whether layout, interaction or language, has to account for the specific context: who the users are, what the business is trying to achieve and the constraints you're working within.

Users: Best for Whom?

Best practices often assume a generic user. But your users are never generic.

- A seasoned professional might want speed and shortcuts.

- A novice may need guidance, reassurance or explanation.

- A person using assistive tech will not interact with your UI the way a mouse user does.

Personas help capture these variations. When done well, they represent real user types with distinct goals, pain points and behavioral patterns, not just demographics. They move the conversation from "users" in the abstract to something more grounded: a frustrated new hire trying to find a single file or a returning customer expecting a fast checkout.

However, personas are often treated as artifacts; a box that gets checked during early research and then largely dismissed or forgotten as the project moves forward. Their true value lies in active reference throughout the design process. They should shape decisions, guide content tone and help arbitrate trade-offs.

Jared Spool puts it plainly:

> "Can every UX team member name one of your users? Can every UX team member describe the differences between users? Can every UX team member describe a user's actual experience?"[1]

If the answer is no, then you're designing in the dark. Real context starts with real people.

Keeping users front and center isn't just about having personas. It's about putting those personas to work on a daily basis, not just during kickoff meetings. Teams should actively refer to specific user types during design reviews and product discussions, grounding their decisions in the needs and behaviors of real people. When user insights are embedded into project management tools, or surfaced in retrospectives and sprint planning, they become part of the operational rhythm, not just documentation that sits on a virtual shelf.

Equally important is reinforcing user context in conversations. Quoting from user interviews, playing short clips in presentations, and repeating core needs or pain points out loud in meetings all help build shared understanding. The goal is to make your users so present in the day-to-day that their voices guide decisions naturally.

This isn't about formality or process hygiene. It's about consistency. It's about cultivating a design culture that resists drifting into assumption or habit. The more visible users are in daily decision-making, the less likely your team will fall back on vague generalizations or "default" UX decisions.

Business Goals: What Are You Actually Optimizing For?

Too often, UX decisions are made in pursuit of a vague metric such as more clicks, faster flows, or higher conversion. But those aren't goals. They are outcomes, and they only matter if they align with what the business actually needs to achieve.

Every product or service exists for a reason beyond usability. UX must serve that purpose—or at least understand it—before applying "best practice" solutions.

Consider how business goals can vary depending on the domain. For example, a nonprofit platform focused on educating the public about climate change may not be interested in maximizing click-through rates. Instead, its success might be measured by how long users stay on the site and how well they understand the material. In that context, information clarity and content depth matter more than streamlining interactions.

Now consider a B2B tool used by financial analysts. Here, data accuracy and auditability might outweigh speed or simplicity. Users need to trust what they see and trace where it came from. A slower, more deliberate interface may be the right choice, even if it may feel contrary to typical best practices around efficiency.

As another example, take an HR portal for employee benefits enrollment. Success here might not be measured by how quickly someone completes a form, but by how confident and informed they feel when making a decision. Rushing users through a streamlined flow may reduce clarity, not improve it.

These aren't edge cases. They're everyday examples of why blindly following best practices can steer you away from what actually matters.

UX Success Depends on Business Alignment

A beautifully minimalist interface that's easy to use might still be a failure if it encourages the wrong behavior, hides critical information, or omits a step needed for compliance. Good UX doesn't just make things easier. It makes the right things easier, in ways that reflect the business's intent and responsibility.

Achieving alignment means starting with clarity. Every feature or flow should be grounded in a specific business objective. Designers and product teams need to understand not just what they're building, but why it matters and what success looks like from the business's point of view. That understanding should guide the structure, interactions and prioritization of the experience itself.

This also requires an understanding of the metrics that matter. Not all measurements are created equal. It's important to distinguish between surface-level engagement numbers and indicators of true business impact. Teams should be able to explain why a specific metric is meaningful and how the design supports it.

And sometimes, alignment means compromise. But not in the sense of watering down design quality. Instead, it may mean prioritizing a business goal over a user need in the short term to unlock future wins. You might launch a feature that satisfies internal metrics before it fully meets user expectations, or accept a temporary friction point to support a revenue objective. These decisions are not ideal, though they can be strategic. They help teams build credibility, secure stakeholder buy-in or keep a project alive. The key is to make these compromises consciously, with a clear plan to shift focus back to the user when the time is right.

Just as you would never design for a generic user, you shouldn't design for generic business goals. Clarity is what ensures you're building the right thing for the right reason.

When business context is ignored, even well-designed experiences can lead to bad outcomes. But when UX decisions are grounded in purpose, even unconventional solutions can succeed.

Constraints: Design Doesn't Happen in a Vacuum

Every project has limits. Some are obvious from the start, others only emerge under pressure. When we overlook these constraints, we risk wasting time and resources, and building something unusable or unshippable. Understanding constraints is not about settling. Rather it's about being thoughtful and strategic.

Constraints generally fall into four primary categories, each with its own implications for design and delivery:

- **Technical**: Your platform may be locked into a legacy CMS. The dev team might only have front-end bandwidth in certain sprints. Mobile responsiveness might be harder than it seems due to embedded tools or third-party dependencies.

- **Organizational**: Multiple departments may be competing for priority or screen space. Legal might have final sign-off. Brand may mandate rigid tone, language or visual requirements.

- **Regulatory**: You may need to comply with HIPAA, GDPR, PCI or other standards that dictate how you handle data, display information or enable user interaction.

- **Financial**: Even the best ideas can be shelved when the budget does not support them. This includes everything from licensing tools to hiring specialists to building and testing advanced interactions.

Some constraints are easy to identify. Others emerge only through experience, often as internal resistance, technical debt or late-stage limitations.

Rather than treating constraints as blockers, use them as design inputs. Take the case of a feature that relies on a third-party API. The API may have rate limits, slow response times, or inconsistent uptime. Rather than waiting for a perfect solution or overengineering a workaround, you might design with these limitations in mind—introducing loading states, caching strategies, or partial results to preserve the experience. The constraint doesn't prevent good UX. In fact, it pushes you to create one that's resilient, transparent, and user-aware.

Consider another scenario where brand or compliance guidelines restrict layout or language choices. Rather than fight these limitations, you can lean into structure and typography to reinforce clarity. The constraint becomes a design challenge worth solving.

And if accessibility guidelines restrict certain interactions, treat that not as a limitation but as a prompt to find more inclusive, effective alternatives.

Constraints like these can steer you toward sharper thinking and stronger outcomes, if you allow them to shape your process instead of resisting them.

Designing with constraints doesn't compromise quality or stifle innovation. Some of the most thoughtful, elegant experiences come from managing limitations wisely, not from boundless freedom. When done right, we can channel our creativity into solutions that work within the realities of our environment while producing something that's thoughtful, effective and truly innovative.

Most importantly, be proactive. Identify constraints early. Ask difficult questions up front. Plan for constraint-driven innovation before your "best practice" ideas get shut down late in the process.

Balancing the Three Contextual Forces

Each contextual factor—users, business goals and constraints—matters on its own. However, their real power comes from how they interact. Design decisions rarely serve just one of these forces. In most cases, you are navigating the tension between them.

A feature that delights users might be too expensive to build right now. A scaled-back or temporary version may need to launch first so that it helps keep the project moving and demonstrates value early. Choosing progress over perfection can be a strategic decision, especially when proving ROI or securing future investment.

A flow that fully supports business goals might still frustrate users if it lacks the necessary context or guidance. That doesn't mean the goal is wrong. It means the experience needs to bridge the gap. Small adjustments like inline help, on-boarding cues or added clarity can pre-serve user trust while still delivering on the business objective.

And sometimes, a constraint that looks like a blocker becomes a catalyst for bet-ter design. Compliance requirements, for example, might initially seem restrictive. But when approached creatively, they can lead to cleaner interactions, stronger com-munication and improved accessibility, of-ten benefiting more users than the rule was designed to protect.

The best UX doesn't come from favoring one factor over the others. It comes from balancing the needs of users, the goals of the business and the realities of the environ-ment. Success lies in making thoughtful, intentional decisions and being able to explain the reasoning behind them.

If something deviates from a best practice yet fits your users, supports your business goals and works within your constraints, that is not a compromise. That is good design.

---

1. Jared Spool, "It's Time We Seriously Talk About Users and Experiences," *UX Collective (Medium)*, November 10, 2020,

   https://uxdesign.cc/its-time-we-seriously-talk-about-users-and-experiences-f0de4daf9259.

Chapter Three

Friction Isn't the Enemy

"Make it frictionless" has become a rallying cry in digital product design. It's often shorthand for user-friendly, efficient and delightful. Somewhere along the way, though, this well-intentioned mantra became a mandate. Every extra click, confirmation or decision point was seen as a barrier to be eliminated. Speed and simplicity became synonymous with good design.

But frictionless isn't always flawless.

The truth is, friction can be valuable. Sometimes, it's essential. It can create space for reflection, reduce errors and guide better decisions. Removing too much friction can erode trust, encourage impulsive actions and strip away moments that give users clarity or confidence.

Consider a one-click donation feature. It's undeniably convenient, but is convenience the right goal when money is changing hands? Shouldn't we want the donor to pause, to make a meaningful connection with their intention, to ensure they're giving the right amount and to feel good about the commitment?

In many cases, the pursuit of a frictionless experience becomes a pursuit of passivity. Users are guided along a path so smooth they don't even realize where it leads. That's not always user-centered. Sometimes, good design means slowing users down just enough to let them stay in control.

Good Friction vs. Bad Friction

Not all friction is created equal. Some of it helps. Some of it hinders. The key is understanding the difference.

Bad friction is the kind that slows users down without offering value. It's the poorly labeled form, the three-step login with no justification, the pop-up that interrupts instead of informs. It's frustrating, confusing and often invisible to the people who built it. This is friction for friction's sake or worse, friction that results from sloppy or thoughtless design.

Good friction, on the other hand, is intentional. It earns its place in the experience by serving a purpose: preventing mistakes, reinforcing trust, encouraging reflection or creating moments of satisfaction and delight. It's the extra confirmation before deleting a file. The gentle nudge to review a cart before checkout. The pause in a donation flow that gives someone time to connect with their values.

Good friction is a signal, not a speed bump. It's the design equivalent of asking, "Are you sure?" or "Have you thought about this?" at exactly the right moment. It's not there to get in the way, but to help users feel confident and informed.

The challenge for product teams isn't to eliminate friction entirely. It's to design it deliberately. Friction should be a tool, not a trap. And when used well, it doesn't slow users down. It helps them move forward with clarity and intention.

***

Case Study:
Amazon's Evolution from Frictionless to Thoughtful

Few companies have been as influential in shaping digital behavior as Amazon. Its 1997 introduction of 1-Click Checkout was a game-changer. By removing nearly all barriers between desire and purchase, it allowed users to buy with a single click using pre-saved information. This became the epitome of frictionless design—and it worked. Amazon saw a notable jump in sales and became synonymous with convenience.

But convenience came at a cost.

The ultra-low-friction flow led to accidental purchases, impulse buying and an increase in order cancellations and returns. The lack of confirmation steps removed critical moments for users to pause and review, Moments that could have prevented frustration and regret.

In 2017, after the patent for 1-Click expired, Amazon quietly replaced it with **Buy It Now**. This change introduced a small but meaningful difference: users were prompted to confirm their shipping and payment details before completing the order. It was a deliberate reintroduction of friction. And it worked, not by increasing effort, but by improving confidence, reducing mistakes and strengthening the overall user experience.

This shift wasn't just a UX decision. It was also a strategic one. While the 1-Click model drove conversions, it also generated substantial licensing revenue from companies like Apple. Once the patent expired, Amazon was free to optimize the experience for customer satisfaction instead of patent profitability.

The lesson is simple. Even the most iconic frictionless design can benefit from slowing things down. In this case, the added friction helped users feel more in control, trust the process more deeply and feel better about their purchase.

Design Perspective:
LESSONS IN INTENTIONAL FRICTION

Design for decision points. Not every flow should be lightning-fast. Some should invite reflection.

Remove mindless convenience. When actions have consequences, make space for users to think.

Friction signals importance. Extra steps show that something meaningful is happening.

UX isn't about fewer clicks. It's about smarter ones. Design the right interactions, not just the fastest path.

Chapter Four
Designing with Awareness, Not Autopilot

Best practices are seductive. They promise certainty, save time and offer a ready-made solution to almost any design problem. However, when we apply them without pausing to reflect, we risk solving the wrong problem beautifully, or worse, embedding the wrong assumption into a product that reaches thousands.

Design isn't copying what worked elsewhere. It's making the *right* choices for *this* moment, *these* users and *this* challenge.

The Autopilot Trap

In fast-paced environments, best practices offer speed. They reduce cognitive load in the design process, lower the barrier to decision-making and carry the weight of credibility. But using them on autopilot often leads to design by muscle memory, where familiarity substitutes for insight.

Just because something worked in another product, or in the last version of yours, doesn't mean it's appropriate now. Familiarity may feel safe, but that comfort can be deceptive.

The Pause That Powers Better Design

Instead of defaulting to a best practice, insert a deliberate pause. Not a slow-down—a check-in.

Ask yourself:

"Am I solving the right problem?"

"Is this solution still relevant?"

"What else might this decision affect?"

Even a five-minute reflection can steer you away from unexamined conventions and toward more thoughtful, tailored outcomes.

Questions to Ask Before Settling for a Best Practice

This is your short internal checklist, an interruption to the reflex.

- **Who are we designing for right now?** Not "users" in the abstract, *this* audience, with *these* constraints and expectations.

- **What are we optimizing for?** Trust? Efficiency? Engagement? Accessibility? The answer should influence the method.

- **What are the known constraints?** Consider technical debt, legal limits, team capability, user device access and time-to-market pressures.

- **Have we tried this before?** Context includes history. Knowing what worked, or failed, in the past can prevent cycles of repeated mistakes.

- **What are the risks of sticking with the norm?** Familiar patterns may cause real friction if they don't align with your product's goals or audience needs.

When Convention Fails

Even the most celebrated patterns can backfire when used without consideration. What worked in one context can fall flat, or even frustrate, in another. That's why it's important to keep our critical thinking sharp, especially when the solution feels too easy or familiar.

Sometimes the "obvious" solution breaks down.

Infinite scroll can create a seamless browsing experience. But it can also bury critical calls to action that would otherwise appear at the end of a page. When users never reach a natural stopping point, they may never encounter key information, forms, or next steps that drive business value.

Modal dialogs can be useful for drawing attention to a single action or message. But when implemented without regard for accessibility, they can block screen readers, trap keyboard navigation, or confuse users who rely on assistive technology to move through a page.

Hamburger menus have become standard on mobile, where screen space is limited. But on desktop layouts with ample room, hiding navigation behind an icon can create unnecessary friction. Users may overlook important sections or features that would be more discoverable in a traditional menu layout.

Each of these patterns is common, but not universally useful. And blindly following the herd can result in disengaged users or inaccessible experiences.

Designing with awareness means being willing to go against the grain when the grain no longer fits the context.

***

Making the Case for Change

When you intentionally deviate from a best practice, you may need to explain your reasoning to stakeholders, other designers or leadership.

Just remember that you're not breaking rules. You're choosing the right approach for the job.

A compelling justification begins with a clear articulation of the goal. What are you trying to accomplish, and why does your chosen approach support that objective better than the familiar default?

Support your decision with evidence. This could be data from usability testing, relevant research, user feedback or even firsthand observations. The stronger the connection between your insight and the design choice, the more credible your reasoning becomes.

Compare your proposed solution with the conventional one. Explain the trade-offs and highlight how your version better fits the specific needs of your context or users.

Finally, outline how you plan to monitor and evaluate the outcome. Whether it's through analytics, A/B testing, user sessions or customer feedback, show that this decision is being made deliberately and that you're prepared to adjust based on what you learn.

Designing on autopilot might get you to launch faster, but it won't guarantee you land in the right place. To design better, pause more, question more and choose your solutions with intention, not just convenience.

Handling Pushback with Credibility and Grace

Even when you've clarified the goal, gathered the evidence and mapped the trade-offs, pushback happens. Sometimes it comes from well-meaning collaborators. Sometimes it comes from a stakeholder or executive sponsor. In either case, your job isn't just to defend the work—it's to translate its value.

Start by aligning with shared outcomes. Frame your rationale in terms that matter to your audience: risk reduction, revenue impact, operational efficiency. Don't just say, "Users are confused." Say, "This confusion could reduce first-time conversions by 15%."

If you're getting resistance from leadership, bring them in early—but keep the ask light. Instead of pushing for full research participation, share a highlight reel or offer a short walkthrough before a standing meeting. A ten-minute story, framed in business terms, can build more buy-in than a full report they'll never read.

When presenting options, avoid framing the conversation as right vs. wrong. Offer multiple paths forward with clear trade-offs:

"Option A meets user expectations and can ship in two sprints. Option B aligns with the executive vision but adds two extra sprints and additional QA."

This positions you as a partner, not a challenger.

And don't underestimate the power of storytelling. A single user quote describing frustration often lands better than a spreadsheet. Human details cut through the noise.

When the Answer Is Still No

Sometimes, despite your best effort, your recommendation won't win. That's okay.

Deliver the chosen version with the same level of care. But keep good records. Document the rationale, the objections and the potential risks. Not to say "I told you so," but so you're ready when results miss the mark.

When that moment comes, respond with:

"Here's what we learned. Here's what we could try next."

That kind of resilience builds trust. Over time, consistent, evidence-backed thinking earns more influence than a single debate ever could.

Design isn't about winning every battle. It's about keeping user value visible, even when you're not the loudest voice in the room.

Chapter Five

The CUE Framework™

A Practical Tool for Intentional Design

Best practices are useful—as long as they align with your situation. So how do you evaluate whether to follow, adapt, or abandon them?

Enter the **CUE Framework**, a lightweight yet powerful tool for design decision-making. It helps you step back, assess the situation holistically and move forward with clarity and intention.

CUE stands for:

Context What's unique about this situation?
Users Who are we designing for and what do they value?
Evidence What do research, metrics, or experience suggest?

These categories aren't silos. Users exist within context, and evidence often reflects both people and situations. Separating them helps you examine each lens with intention, and ensures that no single factor dominates your decision-making. The CUE framework is less about rigid categories and more about creating space for deliberate reflection.

Let's explore each one.

Context: The Constraints and Realities You Can't Ignore

Rather than thinking of context as a list of fixed characteristics, think of it as the stage where your design has to perform. It sets the rules of engagement. Consider what's happening around the user and the system when a decision gets made.

Is the experience playing out on a fast-moving factory floor or in a quiet home office? Is the product new and disruptive, or is it expected to match an existing legacy standard? Is the organization under pressure to convert more users quickly, or to ensure regulatory compliance?

Context is made up of conditions, tensions and expectations that shape the boundaries of good design. It tells you what's at stake, what's allowed and what might be invisible unless you deliberately go looking for it. New products may benefit from onboarding and education, while mature products might prioritize optimization and efficiency.

Users: The People Who Give Design Its Meaning

Every decision you make eventually collides with a person. Not an average user. Not a persona on a slide. A real person with their own context, limitations, habits and expectations. That's why designing with users in mind goes beyond identifying demographics or roles. It means recognizing what they value most in the moments when decisions are made.

Are your users novices who need clarity and confidence, or experts who crave speed and control? Are they multitasking in a loud warehouse or focusing intently at a desk? What's their mental state? Are they exploring, troubleshooting, or under pressure to finish a task?

Design choices that seem minor, like label placement, button language, timing of confirmation messages, can either reinforce a sense of ease or amplify frustration. Best practices often assume the user is just like us. But intentional design asks: who are *they* really, and what do *they* need right now?

Evidence: Replace Assumptions with Insight

The design process is rarely short on opinions, but it should never be short on insight. Evidence grounds your work in reality. It's the compass that keeps your design decisions aligned with how people actually behave, not just how we think they should.

Too often, teams rely on assumptions or anecdotal feedback because it's faster or more comfortable. But evidence doesn't have to mean formal research reports. It can be patterns you notice in user behavior, questions that keep surfacing in support tickets, or friction points identified in usability tests. It might come from analytics, interviews, or even conversations with frontline staff.

What matters is that you're listening. Evidence isn't just about validation. It's discovery. It reveals what's working, what's missing and what's misunderstood. Used well, it transforms opinion-driven design into user-informed strategy.

Using CUE in Practice

The real value of the CUE framework shows up in moments of tension—when you're tempted to default to convention, or when the team is split on how to move forward. It's not a formal process or a template to fill out. It's a mindset check. A way to pause and ask, "Are we designing with our eyes open?"

Use CUE in design critiques to frame feedback around real constraints, real users and real data. Bring it into project kickoffs to align the team on what matters most. Lean on it when justifying decisions to stakeholders, especially when your choices deviate from common patterns.

Whether you're auditing an existing experience or building something from scratch, CUE helps you zoom out before you zoom in. It doesn't add steps. It adds clarity.

Designing by CUE, Not by Default

The CUE framework empowers you to design with nuance. It invites you to trade certainty for curiosity, and prescription for perception. It's a way of checking your instincts without shutting them down.

When you apply CUE, you're not just choosing a pattern, you're making a case. You're weighing constraints, honoring real people and letting the evidence guide your next move. It's not a matter of reinventing the wheel with every project. It's making sure the wheel fits the terrain.

Good design isn't about what usually works. It's about what works *here*, *now*, *for these people*. That's the shift: from designing by default to designing with intent.

Be sure to check the end of the book for access to exclusive CUE Framework™ resources.

Conclusion
Designing for Clarity

If there's one thread that runs through every chapter in this book, it's this: good design isn't about doing what's common. It's about doing what's right.

"Best practices" can be useful guides, but they're not the finish line. They're a baseline. A starting point. Tools in a much larger toolbox. When we rely on them too heavily, we risk designing for hypotheticals instead of the humans in front of us. We sacrifice insight for efficiency. We choose familiarity over proper fit.

Designing for nuance means resisting that temptation. It means choosing to engage with the messy, layered, human reality of every product, every problem, every context. It's about staying in the uncomfortable space where answers aren't immediate and trusting that clarity will emerge through the process, not in spite of it.

It also means embracing iteration not as a failure to get it right the first time, but as a commitment to getting it better *every* time. Good design isn't static. It evolves. It's a living conversation between the designer, the user, the system and the moment in which all three intersect.

And that conversation requires listening.

It requires humility. Curiosity. A willingness to say, "I don't know yet, but I'll find out."

Because that's the real work. Not replicating patterns from someone else's playbook, but learning to see patterns in the wild and then shaping them with intent.

So as you move forward in your practice, here's what I hope you carry with you:

Design for clarity, not convention.

Convention is comfortable. But clarity is powerful.

Clarity invites trust. Clarity removes doubt. Clarity puts users first, especially when it requires breaking from what's expected.

Don't chase shortcuts. Chase understanding. Don't design for what's typical. Design for what's *true*.

And when in doubt, return to your foundations:

- **Context** matters.

- **Users** matter.

- **Evidence** matters.

That's where great design lives. Not in the rules, but in the reasoning.

Get the Free Companion Resources

Access exclusive downloadable tools to help you design with more clarity, context and confidence.

Here's what's included:

The CUE Framework Resource Set – A visual summary of core principles and common pitfalls—plus printable and fillable one-page worksheets to guide intentional UX decisions.

PDF version of *Better than Best Practices* – A searchable, portable version of the book—ideal for quick reference, digital note-taking, and on-the-go reading.

Just scan the QR code below.

propulsionux.com/btbp

About the author

A. Robert Hinson (known to his peers as Bobby) is a strategic UX consultant with over 25 years of experience spanning user experience, product development, web design and visual communication. He's the founder of Propulsion UX, a consultancy that helps teams design and build digital products with clarity and purpose. Throughout his career, He has led initiatives across industries and guided teams through complex design challenges—always focused on aligning user needs, business goals and technical realities.

www.ingramcontent.com/pod-product-compliance
Lightning Source LLC
Chambersburg PA
CBHW071508210326
41597CB00018B/2703